CHARLES DEBENHAM'S EAST ANGLIA

First published in 2000 by Sansom & Company Ltd.,
81g Pembroke Road, Bristol BS8 3EA

Tele: 0117 9737207
Facsimile: 0117 9238991
e.mail: johnsansom@aol.com

Copyright:

images Charles Debenham
text David Buckman

ISBN 1 900178 92 3

First publication of this book coincided with an exhibition
of the artist's work at the Chappel Galleries, Chappel

British Cataloguing-in-Publication Data
A catalogue record for this book is available from The British
Library

Typeset by Mayhew Typesetting, Rhayader, Powys
Printed by Hackman Print, Tonypandy

CHARLES DEBENHAM'S
EAST ANGLIA

David Buckman

Sansom &
Company

THE BULL HOTEL, *COLCHESTER*
This was done in the early 1960s. The newspaper and tobacconist's that you can see under the sign at the left was well-known to me. Every morning from the ages of 10 to 20 I began my morning paper-round there. We would gather at about a quarter to seven and the round would take just under the hour, on a bike. It was my only regular source of income, throughout my student days.

ST JULIAN GROVE, *COLCHESTER*
This was done in 1997. The association that I have with the Grove is that my friend Norman Warner used to live next to the pink house, where his family grew up. Norman's story was that as a child he and the son of the lady in the pink house were playing with some water in the front room and spilt some of it. They decided to mop it up, the friend calling out: "Hey, mum, there's a pattern on this lino!"

Few artists are better qualified to depict East Anglia, its buildings, its people, its character and quirks than Charles Debenham. When in 1996 the Chappel Galleries held an exhibition of Debenham's outdoor paintings of Essex and Suffolk towns, and published a wallet of colour cards of them, many people for the first time heard of an artist who had quietly and diligently recorded the face of his region for over 40 years. It takes Debenham's peculiar dedication each Christmas Day to set off whatever the weather and paint, for hours, a bleak seaside town, a deserted railway station or what to anyone else would seem just another row of suburban houses.

On the occasion of the 1996 Chappel Galleries show, another fine but very different East Anglian painter, Roderic Barrett, drew attention to "the afffectionate care" with which Debenham approached his "fascinating discoveries", producing "paintings to live with". This work was "a celebration of the ordinary. Not for Charles Debenham the noble architectural structures or the quaint preserved, but the kind of street that may be seen in many local towns and villages. Houses jumbled together, often with no sense of order, filling whatever space happened to be there, roof shapes, window sizes, lodged there by the aimlessness of history and the best efforts of various jobbing builders, or stationary rows of houses, all much the same except for the telling colour of a door, the gate that is different."

Barrett noted that it was "these very ordinary characters which capture Charles Debenham and through his art engage us. Each painting encourages us to pause, begin to absorb all that there is there, enjoy the individuality of the commonplace. Here are these gates, bridges, roads and houses, separate from us, indifferent to our presence yet possessing when looked at by an artist all manner of sad, amazing, moving, unexpectedly telling juxtapositions. There is nothing phoney in these paintings, they are quite free of arty affections. This is a singular gift."

Charles Debenham was born in Colchester, in 1933. He lives in Great Horkesley, near the town, the geography and history of which continue to fascinate him. After St John's Green Junior School he attended Colchester Royal Grammar School. He remembers being "good at art, but useless at maths, physics and chemistry." Aged only 14, Charles began evening classes at Colchester School of Art, which eased him into the work mode of a provincial art school. Debenham was full-time there from 1948 to 1953. He trained as an illustrator and was fortunate in having as principal John O'Connor, then in his early forties and establishing a national reputation as an illustrator, painter and printmaker. At first, Charles concentrated on wood engraving. He benefited from the tuition of that master of the technique, Blair Hughes-Stanton, a Venice Biennale international prize winner, who was to become such an influential teacher at major London art schools. Charles was taught painting by Hugh Cronyn and Carel Weight, shortly after to start a long, legendary term as professor of painting at the Royal College of Art, a Royal Academician whose almost surreal interpretation of the ordinary was to prove so different from Debenham's.

Charles feels that he was fortunate in his time at Colchester Art School, as "the average age there was over 20, with people being demobbed from the forces. I was taken from a teenage, all-male society into a predominantly female and much older one. It put years on you, in the nicest sense." Colchester was a small school, totalling about 35 students, painters and illustrators intermingling for life classes. Specialist classes might be only half-a-dozen strong. Before he was 11 years old Debenham had started a paper round seven days a week. At art school that remained his main income source, supplemented later by an Essex County Major Award, "sufficient for me to have to pay for my own exams."

As a counter-balance to art, Charles joined the local Church Lads' Brigade physical training team. It was an interest that continued until he left art school, although by that time the compulsory church parades and church attendance had made him change allegiance, when he was old enough, to the local youth club. There the standard was much higher.

LADIES' LOO
BUTT ROAD, COLCHESTER

COLD NIGHT, *HEADGATE, COLCHESTER*
This is another early-1960s picture.
Headgate was originally the main gate out
of Colchester, through the Roman wall on
to the road to London.

The Bull Hotel, on the left, has not
changed much, but the lovely curved front
of the tobacconist's with its dominating
poster has now been rebuilt: flat, dull and
uninteresting.

GENTS HAIRDRESSING, *COLCHESTER*
This is a scene at North Bridge,
Colchester, painted in the mid-1980s. Mr
Elliott's is now a sandwich bar. His barber's
shop was situated between the old cattle
and poultry markets.

It was aged about 15 and attending evening classes that
Debenham had his first encounter with one of the greats of East
Anglian art. "My teacher, Bill Judge, who looked like a friendly
Mussolini and painted illustrations for book covers, advised: 'More
sketching.' He lodged at Dedham, so I cycled over to begin my
sketching there. I thought I was getting along all right, but my first
over-the-shoulder critic, an old chap, just muttered something,
continued on his way, then returned and asked if I would like to see
some of his paintings. The studio was filled with lots of studies of
horses, I later told Bill. 'You were honoured,' he said. The old artist
was Sir Alfred Munnings," the controversial president of the Royal
Academy.

Five years at Colchester Art School provided Debenham with his
NDD, National Diploma in Art and Design, and aged 21 he joined an
advertising firm. "It was very humbling. I remember going to London
for my first job interview, climbing many stairs to an attic studio. I was
confident, as I felt that I could draw anything put in front of me, but
the man interviewing me said: 'Can you draw palm trees?' Of course,
I had never sat in front of a palm tree. Naively, it had never occurred
to me that you might have to draw off-the-cuff. Thus, I got my edges
knocked off."

Still in his early twenties, Debenham set up his own studio in
Colchester. It enabled him to "move into public information, selling
ideas rather than things." This involved providing major designer
services for bodies such as Anglian Water, the National Rivers
Authority later known as the Environment Agency, British Telecom
and the Central Electricity Generating Board. After the agency,
Charles worked briefly in a display manufacturing partnership as a
designer. Eventually, he chose to work entirely by himself, providing
educational and environmental design services, the National Grid and
National Power among his clients. School children, disabled groups
and people with learning difficulties are key aspects of that work.

Charles' work has meant extensive overseas travel. One interesting job in the late 1970s involved creating a huge exhibition pavilion in Cairo for Bowater's. He remembers the experience as "fabulous. A director of Bowater's and I were treated as VIPs at the airport, without the need to pass through customs. We entered Cairo in a limousine with a motorcycle escort with sirens wailing and at the hotel were given red carpet treatment. I never opened the door for myself all the time I was there. It was an introduction to a completely different culture. I had expressed an interest in genuine Oriental dancing, but it did come as rather a surprise when our hosts took over a night club to entertain just the two of us. Seated on huge cushions in the middle of the floor gave me a unique understanding of this traditional ancient art."

Charles recalls a singular event during his many drives between Cairo and Alexandria, on the Egyptian coast. "Conditions in the country were then desperately poor. Before we started for Alexandria, the driver would take his Mercedes round to the garage where they cut a new tyre tread with a hacksaw. Off we would speed into the desert, with me spending the entire journey fingers crossed hoping that the tyres would hold out. I remember one journey when we saw, on the shimmering horizon, what appeared to be a light being turned on and off, like someone flicking a cigarette lighter. As we approached, we saw it was a petrol tanker on fire with the driver sitting astride the tank attempting to beat out the flames coming from one of the hatches with his headdress. We decided to put our foot down. On the way back, all we could see was a huge circle of melted tar – no sign of the tanker!"

Debenham's Cairo pavilion won top prize. As a result, the United States government asked him to design for it in Europe. The ensuing work in the early 1980s for America's Department of Agriculture called for trans-Atlantic travel for demonstrations and briefings, resulting in displays in France, Switzerland and the UK. The Cairo pavilion also led

to another exhibition pavilion for that much more orthodox Arab country, Saudi Arabia, with rather alarming consequences.

Much of Charles' Saudi work involved clearing things through customs. While on one such documentation trip, he noticed a huge peninsula of wood chips by the harbour at Jedda, where dhows were still being constructed by hand. His companion for the pavilion job, Isa, an Arab speaker, said that she would like to photograph the scene, and they returned the following day before their normal work started. Crossing the multi-lane road system afterwards, Charles glanced back to see Isa with two men hanging onto her on the central reservation. Returning to help her, fearing that she was being robbed, they were both soon surrounded by a gathering crowd of very excited men.

"Hearing sirens and seeing uniformed men arrive, I thought: 'At last, we are going to be rescued.' Then I had a rifle butt slammed into me, and I was out cold. Next, we were in the back of a truck being taken in for questioning. It seemed that the two men who had originally held Isa were plain-clothes policemen. They thought that she was taking photographs which were politically and militarily sensitive because of the Arab states' relationship with Israel. After an embarrassing search, we were asked a lot of questions but we were not allowed to speak, we had to write down all our replies. We were not allowed to contact

MONTAGUE BURTON'S NIGHT-TIME VIEW, *COLCHESTER*
Painted mid-winter 1961, standing in one of those old-style recessed windows of Montague Burton's, the men's outfitters. A well lit spot with the advantage of being able to warm your hands on the window glass.

One of Debenham's larger "canvases" measuring 5 by 20 metres, being erected by workmen at Blackpool pleasure beach. A commission from Manx Cable Company, it was part of the town's year 2000 illuminations.

DURRANT, MONUMENTALIST, *COLCHESTER*
This is a summer picture, done in the mid-1960s, and would be unrepeatable because of development. The title is taken directly from the signboard above the window. Durrant's St Mary's Works – now long gone – used to make all the local gravestones and memorials. Probably a lot of their trade came from St Mary's Hospital (the old spike) next door.

our embassy. The situation looked grim until I remembered an invitation to meet the editor of one of Saudi's leading newspapers. I requested that they notified him that we would not be able to keep the appointment. This proved the best ploy possible, because luckily he came and got us out."

Among the more prestigious jobs that Debenham has handled is the London International Boat Show, involving a lot of travelling. His designs for the central feature, around and in the pool, have recreated scenes from the Balearic Isles, Guernsey and Alderney, the Western Isles of Scotland and Ayrshire, the British Inland Waterways and Malta. The most fun jobs were definitely designing the humorous floats for the Lord Mayor's Show, giant mobile figures of housewife hens, costermonger pigs, Europa and John Bull on 40-foot trailers flanked by teams of costumed walkers. "I always took part in the parades. I loved the interaction with the crowds. I would not have missed it for the world!"

Over the years, Debenham has learned to tailor his displays for all types and ages of people. His work for the National Grid, for example, is mainly environmental and educational. "Nature trails have an education centre within them, and these must cater for school parties, people with learning difficulties and disabled groups as well as all the other visitors." It was through the National Grid that he met the television personality Johnny Ball, which led to his designing The Johnny Ball All Electric Roadshow for kids, among other collaborations.

An unusual client that Debenham has worked for is St Paul's, in London. He designed an exhibition on the life of the cathedral. "I had known it previously only as a tourist. Initially, I had to meet the Dean and Chapter. I was naturally more than a little nervous, about meeting them and about the commission. Christopher Wren said of St Paul's: 'If you seek my monument, look around you'. This gives you an awful sense of responsibility. I was plonking something right in the middle of his monument. I tried to design an exhibition that did not interrupt the view as you looked up the ambulatory, and decided that back-angled illuminated screens that blended into the sides, seen only when you came level, would be best. It worked well, and I received many compliments at the opening ceremony."

This was the first occasion on which Charles met the Queen Mother, and they had a chat about what he had done. "I hope that your grandson would approve," said Debenham. The Queen Mother walked on, paused, came back and said: "He is very interested in these things, and I think he would approve of what you've done, but I'll have a word with him." After that, in 1991, Debenham had to prepare an exhibition, in the cathedral's crypt, to celebrate the tenth wedding anniversary of Charles and Diana. "In 1994, when we went to take it out, we could hardly get to it, it was so popular, absolutely packed. I had the royal wedding at St Paul's in my shed for about two years."

Debenham has never made a distinction between this public work, often on a large scale, and his own, often quite small, paintings of East Anglia and elsewhere. "They are both equally demanding and I'm equally proud – if that's the right word – of the two. They all require thought, they have the same sort of problems and all demand your best."

The East Anglian pictures have continued from art school days out with his sketch-book. The liking for architectural features and oddities is long-standing, too. "I was always fascinated by Canaletto's wonderfully detailed grand views. I am now less influenced by them. I've drawn Colchester High Street, which could be called a grand view, many times. My interest now is more to focus on specific details. I'm not seeking to repeat what the architecture looks like, but the effect on it of, say, time, a succession of owners or the planning authorities."

Painting outside, not in a studio, Debenham is always aware of physical factors that will govern the feasibility of completing a picture. "Quite often I see views that I would love to paint, but there is no way that I can position myself to do so. You have to choose a subject where you can remain for a long period. If, like some artists, you take a photograph and work it up later, you can stand briefly in the middle of the street. The way that I work, you can't do that. I need what I call a defensible position, to minimise the risk of pedestrian or vehicle interference if you put an easel up. I need to be able to survive over a number of weeks in a certain spot. Light is another important requirement, not on the subject, but on me. If the sun comes round and hits you straight on, you can't see a thing, and it's time to wash my brushes."

ST BOTOLPH'S CORNER, *COLCHESTER*
This is another view of early-1960s Colchester, done in the summer. The Woolpack Hotel and Empire Restaurant, which form the main part of the picture, are now long-gone, replaced by a huge roundabout. The poster hoarding covered where a bomb-damaged shop used to be. The men are coming out of The Britannia Engineering works, itself another World War Two bombing casualty.

NELSON COTTAGES, *MALDON ROAD, COLCHESTER*
I painted this not far from Colchester town centre in the early 1990s. I was initially attracted by the passageway. Then I realised that the house was built at such really weird angles, with a little triangular yard or garden, and so on. Look at the cornerwork, and the red painting on the lower part of the house, small features which make it such a simple and interesting scene.

"My old friend Roderic Barrett has contrasted the approaches of Matisse and Braque. Matisse insisted that he had to have a clear vision of the whole composition from the start, Braque claiming that a painting 'makes itself under the brush'. Roderic, who paints in the studio, prefers the Matisse approach, and reckons that Braque 'was telling a fast one'. But to me, working on the spot, Braque's statement makes complete sense. I find that paintings do make themselves."

An East Anglian artist admired by Debenham is Edward Seago. He has long been out of favour with many of the more sniffy art critics, but his consistently strong public following has laid his style open to copying. Charles remembers some years ago going to buy some art materials in a local shop. The owner, who was having his coffee break in the back store-room, asked whether he would like a cup. "There was not a door to the store-room, just a curtain pulled across. As we were drinking our Nescafé the curtain parted, two large chaps stood in the entrance slightly behind two easels that flanked the opening and they identified themselves as members of the Fine Art Fraud Squad. They started off with some bizarre questions, such as: 'Has there lately been a run on cerulean blue paint?' 'No.' Several other colour questions followed, all answered by the proprietor in the negative. Then: 'Have there been requests for books on local artists?' 'No' again. It all seemed a bit clumsy. Then they came clean, and it emerged that they were looking for someone forging Seago paintings. Evidently Seago had used a lot of the colours named, so they had concluded that whoever was knocking out the fakes must be buying similar colours by the gallon. Having drawn a blank, the police departed. What was killing me was that there on the two easels were two beautiful seascapes with glorious cerulean blue skies; diplomatically I did not look at the signatures."

Debenham admits to getting a lot of public reaction to his own pictures during their creation. "As you are in the street, you are getting other people's comments all the time. You don't have to wait until the finished painting is in a gallery. They are passing remarks at stage one, stage two, and so on. Their comments can be trying, such as: 'Are you still on the same picture?' or, 'I know where there is a nice scene'. But they can be positive. 'Why are you painting that?' leads you to question why you are, and you should be able to tell them."

GENERAL STORES, *CANTERBURY ROAD, COLCHESTER*
This was painted in the 1970s, my corner-shop
period. Most locations, like my paintings, have
now changed hands.

The average number of sessions on site is about 10, but it can take more. Thus, painting pictures away from home at locations in Norfolk, for his Chappel Galleries exhibition in 2000, proved a lengthy business, with such considerations as position, weather, light and sometimes a 100-mile-plus round trip to be taken into account. Before breakfast every morning Charles takes time to appraise what he is working on, placing it on a chair or in a frame. This might last 30 minutes or so. "I ask myself: 'What do I do next?' After they have been finished a few weeks, they get dragged out again. If a minor alteration is needed, that is the only time I work in the studio. If bits are very bad, they get scraped out and I go back on site again."

Although he has worked on canvas, Debenham routinely chooses board for practical reasons. "This came about mainly through painting abroad. Canvases did not travel easily in a suitcase, so I prefer the small boards. The boards are now a standard 10 by 8 inches, so they all fit one frame size. It may not be high art, but it's practical. The boards are covered with two coats of rabbit-skin size, one brushed on one way, the other the other way, and I paint direct on to that."

Before painting he does "a very crude pencil drawing, in which I confirm with myself that I want to paint what I'm stuck in front of. If it does not work on the sketch it is best to move on, and not waste your time. The drawing, which can be on anything, from a Sainsbury's receipt to the back of a parking ticket, is concerned with the relationship of various shapes. All painting is getting the subject into your head and understanding it.

"The sketch enables me to start work on the sized board, drawing in a thin mix of Payne's Grey. I start with the focal point and work out from that. With luck, the parameters come up the same as on the sketch. By now I have normally managed to accidentally rub out most of the bits I started with, but the faint image is perfect for redrawing in a freer style. The drawing usually takes me between four to six hours, the first dozen or so lines probably accounting for about half that time. After a couple of days for the drawing to dry I normally start by painting the sky and that determines the mood of the painting and restricts my subsequent visits to days with similar weather."

The Debenhams have two dogs and eight cats, including a number of "cat lodgers". Charles insists that when he takes his dog, Alice, a Grand Bleu de Gascogne, "a sort of French bloodhound", on one of their minimum-three-mile walks painting is not thought about. "Alice's time is hers."

CHANGING THE SKY-LINE, *COLCHESTER*
This is a quick sketch which I did when they were constructing the ring road around Colchester in 1975. It was a time when they were gutting the old centre to build a town square of the ubiquitous toytown, building-block variety.

CHRISTMAS DAY, BRADFIELD CHURCH
This was another one of my many Christmas Day painting excursions. It was painted in 1989 in Bradfield, a village near the Stour estuary.

The view of the church is from the forecourt of the pub opposite. I can assure you that there were more customers behind me than in front of me!

Firmly allocated for painting, however, are Christmas and Boxing Days, a habit which stems from Debenham's student years. "Sketchbooks were always due in for mid-term exams. You realised about Christmas-time that they were not quite as full as they should be, so you had to work through your holidays to complete them. I concluded that if I could draw on Christmas Day I could be selfish enough to be an artist. Oddly, Boxing Day 1999 was the first missed that I can remember, I got a tyre shredded halfway to site. After that I did paint on Millennium Day. I know that record will not be equalled for another thousand years."

Debenham admits also to "only going on holiday to paint", adding wryly: "you might wonder how I've remained married." Despite his slow and meticulous preparation, away from home, "I normally manage a couple of full paintings and several knock-in, sketch-type pictures." Although it was going away that prompted him to use boards, "I always want to paint on a canvas, because it is nice and big. You can splosh the paint on." Now he has come to appreciate the speed with which the brush covers small areas of board, without having to mix up a lot of paint. Keeping control of a large canvas outdoors can also present problems. He is not happy with acrylics or watercolour, reckoning that "it's a lot harder to paint a good watercolour than a good oil. I make a lot of mistakes which I have to correct, which I wouldn't have a dog's chance of correcting in watercolour." As at home, painting outside abroad presents many hazards. A memorable one for Charles was being aggressively propositioned by a generously proportioned young Spanish lady on an escarpment overlooking Malaga Cathedral (a free offer, as it turned out, the girl being sponsored by some local lads he had met while painting). Being too busy with the brush, it was an offer he declined.

Debenham began exhibiting with Colchester Art Society when still a student. It had been founded in 1946 and when Charles was included in its Fifty Years Anniversary Exhibition, at Chappel Galleries, in 1996, it was a roll-call of modern British painting, names ranging from John Aldridge, Edward Bawden and Robert Buhler to Humphrey Spender, Kenneth Rowntree and Carel Weight. Charles, now one of the most senior members, remembers the early days when most were professional painters and exhibitions were held in Colchester Castle. There were informal meetings in the Marquis of Granby pub on North Hill, where such luminaries as Cedric Morris, Arthur Lett-Haines and John Nash would rub shoulders. The painter Lucy Harwood sticks especially in Debenham's mind. "Whenever a subject was put to the vote, everyone would look to see whether Cedric and John had put their hands up, then all hands went up. On one occasion all hands went up as usual, including that of Lucy, who turned to Morris and said: 'What are we voting for, Cedric?'" Later, with the arrival of The Minories as a gallery, there would be several Society shows in the year. One annual exhibition of which Debenham is fond is the Royal West of England Academy show, in Bristol, to which he has been a regular contributor ever since fellow-artist Dione Page suggested he took part. "It is one of the nicest shows that you could go in. The place, scale and attitudes all seem to be just right. I love it." Another favoured venue is the South West Academy, inaugurated in Exeter in 2000, where Charles showed two pictures. He enjoys seeing other artists' work. "I love most paintings, often looking at a picture and saying: 'I wish I had painted that.'"

Debenham has long contributed to the Royal Academy (RA) Summer Exhibition. Many thousands of artists submit in the hope of getting one of the limited number of spaces, and Royal Academicians have priority. Even if a non-Academician has work selected it may not be hung, and even if it is hung it may not be on the line in a prominent place but skied almost out of view. Debenham first showed in 1980, and both pictures were sold. Since then, he has found the RA "a great lottery".

It was the RA show that provided one of Debenham's most odd meetings with a client. The picture bought was *Outside Jobs*, shown at Burlington House in 1990. "In the picture old Reg Williams, at Edwardstone, is shown working in his garden, his outside loo in the background. The reason for my painting it was the outside loos. They have always fascinated me. My grandma Lily Debenham, over at Long Melford, had a double-seater: one adult and one child-size. If the baker's visit coincided with her call of nature, orders and gossip were exchanged via the well-ventilated door. In the middle of painting my picture, Reg's cat, Splodge – really the cat from next door that had

adopted Reg, after his owner the artist Ed Middleditch had died – came along and took centre stage and gave real meaning to the title.

"When I went round for a final look at the Academy show, I noticed a scratch on the picture. According to the purchase slip, it had been bought by a David P Frost. I phoned up and suggested to the woman at the other end of the line that, rather than the buyer collecting it, I would pick it up, repair and return it. When the repair was done, I rang up again and said that it was ready. She suggested that I took it into Mr Frost's office, although I was a bit reluctant, as I thought that having a picture delivered there might get him into trouble. Had he got a secretary I could leave it with? There were a lot of odd responses while all this was going on. Anyway, I agreed to deliver. When I took the picture along in a carrier bag, I offered to leave it with the girl at the reception desk, but she insisted that the buyer wanted a word with me. Up I went in the lift, and out of an office came David Frost, of television fame.

"I felt a bit of a fool for not realising who it was in the first place. David Frost had bought an earlier picture of mine. I had recognised the name, but not the person!"

THE BREWERY, *EAST HILL, COLCHESTER*
Exhibited: Royal Academy Summer Exhibition, 1983

Charles' work has brought him into contact with many other celebrities, "again, often with me not knowing who they were." They include the writer A P Herbert, composer Lionel Bart and the comedian Barry Humphries, famous as Dame Edna Everage. Patrick Macnee, better known as John Steed in the cult television series *The Avengers*, Debenham remembers as "a real gent. Sitting next to him at lunch, he removed the bones from my smoked trout for me. Killing time before another engagement, I took him to my local. Nobody could believe that it was Steed, not with Charles."

The launch of the first Co-op Superstore outside Colchester saw Charles entertaining and being entertained by The Comedians, from another television series, funsters such as Frank Carson, Jim Bowen and Bernard Manning. "Whether it was killing time in the store-room or drinking in the pub, they were always on stage."

Charles still relishes one of his own moments of celebrity. Commissioned by Bowater's to furnish a rather grand apartment in Cairo, he attended a high-powered briefing in London. "We had left their splendid premises in Berkeley Square – 'we' being Lord Erroll of Hale, the chairman, and two other lords, and as we entered Harrods our party was greeted by: 'Good morning, Mr Debenham, what can we do for you today?' Explanation: the chap in the tails used to run our local delicatessen – but I didn't tell the lords that!"

Charles making a point to the writer A P Herbert at a private view in 1968.

Debenham drawn by fellow-artist Andrew Dodds.

WILLY LOTT'S NEIGHBOUR, *GUN HILL, DEDHAM*

Welcome to Constable country! Every English art lover has heard of John Constable, Dedham the village where he went to school and Willy Lott's cottage, by Flatford Mill, where *The Haywain* was painted. Not quite so well known or appreciated is this view which has, nevertheless, been the subject of much local discussion. Oddly, only a few of us can see the beauty hidden here. Where else can you find a breaker's yard with Gothic windows and tyre sculptures to rival Carl André's famous Tate Gallery bricks?

There is a treasure-house inside, too. I spent a lunch break sitting on an old seat from the back of a 1940s bus, stroking the ears of a very large woolly Alsatian. Everything in there was a happy third marriage of things that did not quite fit, although it had excellent ventilation. Here was one place where I did not feel overdressed, blending perfectly with my hosts.

The picture was painted in 1999 parked across the road from the scrapyard. Ironically, work was frequently interrupted by salesmen using that stretch of the road demonstrating the performance capabilities of Porches.

Exhibited: South West Academy, 2000

GUN HILL
GARAGE
DEDHAM

Chas Debenham

PARTRIDGE'S, TOY DEPARTMENT, *HADLEIGH*

At one time, Partridge's was 'the' trader in Hadleigh, selling virtually everything. I painted this little corner of their empire in the 1990s. Partridge's like Barclay's have closed a few branches since.

Hadleigh is a lovely place, with strong local artistic connections. Just up the road is Benton End, where Sir Cedric Morris and Lett Haines ran The East Anglian School of Painting and Drawing. Cedric was a great plantsman, a notable bird and flower painter, president of the Colchester Art Society when I was chairman. We used to hatch splendid plots together. He was a lovely man with silver hair, a red kerchief and a twinkle in his eye. When you visited the house, which went back to the sixteenth century, you had to pick your way through corridors full of pictures about 10 deep.

PECULIAR ROW, *MONKS ELEIGH*

At first you think there is symmetry, then you realise that everything is different and yet the same in this group of buildings. Where you think there is balance, there isn't. Note that the dog-tooth pattern in the grey brick is at the top on one bit and on the bottom on the other. Look at the stonework of the lintels over the doors: one is rounded, the other is a triangle.

There is not one window in this whole group that is the same as another. It looks like the builder recreated his local rugby club's colours with a job-lot of stuff from a clearance sale.

As I stood there, I spotted one of those weird coincidences that sometimes occur. If you look at the bottom right-hand corner you see a stone slab. That used to be the base of a petrol pump, which probably disappeared in the 1930s. Now the present owners have put up one of those house name plaques shaped just like the top of the old-style pump. It could be the ghost of the garage that used to be there.

NORFOLK COTTAGES, *NEAR NORTH WALSHAM*

I have forgotten the exact location of these cottages, but they were somewhere near North Walsham. We had hired one of those seaside homes at Walcott for a week. I think the resident of the dog house was on his holidays, too, as I never saw him during the days that I painted it.

While I was painting, my wife Eilish was left with Jessie and Oliver, our two big woolly Bouvier dogs. Jessie particularly liked this bit of the coast and developed a sort of Evel Knievel skill in hurling herself off the cliff into the soft sand.

Evel Knievel, the famous stunt man, remember him?

Exhibited: Royal Academy Summer Exhibition, 1986

GRAND HOTEL, RETIRED, *FRINTON-ON-SEA*

The Grand Hotel, Frinton, was once one of the plushiest of the plush. Frinton is that genteel resort where, when I was painting in 1999, there was a great row going on about whether it should or should not have its first pub. Frinton's proud boast had always been that it was the town without one. The Grand Hotel represented what Frinton stood for in more ways than one. The fact that it is no longer an hotel says everything about the slowly changing face of Frinton.

My painting companion, the artist Andrew Dodds, remembers visiting the Grand as a very young man, when he was courting. The young lady's parents, trying to find out what sort of chap their daughter was associating with, took him to tea at the Grand, where his memory is that they had tutti-frutti.

The Grand is very substantial, commanding a huge greensward. At first, I thought that I would paint it from the front. The problem is that such pictures too easily become seaside picture postcards. Then, I realised that if I went round the side, where the balconies make that lovely curved shape, I could also emphasize the huge emptiness of the scene with its dull grey sky and cold quiet sea.

Although the Grand was a retirement home when I painted it last winter, a recent visit showed that it is now undergoing another change of use. "*A QUALITY CONVERSION,*" announced the notice outside. "*20 PRESTIGIOUS AND WELL-APPOINTED APARTMENTS, MANY WITH BALCONY OR PATIO WITH SEA VIEWS.*"

It did not mention Frinton's most recent attraction, its first pub, The Lock and Barrel.

Chas Debenham

Chas Debenham

MARITIME BUILDINGS, *HARWICH*

These three-storey, mirror-image Victorian fishermen's cottages see you before you see them. My affection for numbers 1 and 2 Little Church Street seems to be shared by former residents, such as Dilys, who remembers during her tenure showing round people who had turned up to see the place where they were born or grew up.

The house where she lived once housed a family with eleven girls and one boy. There was an outside loo, which was convenient for returning sailors, and on such occasions the girls were instructed to: "Keep your eyes away to the wall!"

Dilys remembered the arrival of the boat seen in the picture, which is in the garden of the property known as Admiral's Ballroom. It has probably seen the last of the sea, still under a rusting awning patiently awaiting its refit.

Oh – that dog in the picture, I can put it on the record that it never once missed the white post.

Exhibited: Royal West of England Academy, 1998

ADMIRAL'S BALLROOM *HARWICH*

The companion-piece to *Maritime Buildings*. My informant on that picture, former resident Dilys, kept referring to the Admiral's Ballroom as we talked.

It turned out to be the subject of this view, which is just a change-of-head-angle away from the maritime buildings of the other picture. The name Admiral's Ballroom appealed to me, as did the propped-up verandah with its filled-in end. The boat awaiting renovation, seen in the companion picture, is to the left of the open gate. Despite its more glamorous past, the building has had a chequered history, parts at times having been used for stables, potting shrimps and as a Welsh Chapel.

MRS SMITH'S WASHING, *SUDBURY*

I was first attracted to the front of the terrace where the Smiths live. It has one of those tunnel arrangements that give access to the back, but when I went into it I saw this marvellous workshop. Just then the sun disappeared and it started to spit with rain, but I decided that in the tunnel I could paint protected from both. Another bonus came when one of the many curious over-the-shoulder visitors turned out to be the vicar from the church across the road. It had its own car park, so there would be no more lugging the easel and gear all the way from the municipal car park. "G.A.R. SMITH CARPENTER & JOINER" says the peeling sign board on the workshop. A hint of a past sideline to the business is in the lily device on the plaque over the door of the building with the fading green door, to the right. Today, the workshop sees more of motor-cycle parts.

One day, as she was pushing her bike through her wrought-iron gateway, Mrs Smith pointed at the part of my painting with the unfinished porch. "Years ago I was told by my future mother-in-law: 'If you marry him you'll be all right for jobs around the house.'" Then, glancing at the porch, she added, in a quiet voice, "One day he'll finish it."

Exhibited: Royal West of England Academy, 1999

Chas Deber

THREE WEEKS TO THE NEW SEASON, *ST OSYTH*

This is St Osyth, by the Essex saltings, where a couple of workmen and a foreman on a mobile phone are working fast to refurbish an amusement arcade before the new holiday season. They did not show their faces outside too often, and then just to throw waste into the skips. What attracted me to this scene was its resemblance to a Victorian travelling fair, rows of caravans with gaudy pictures on huge sheets of canvas doubling the impact.

The neon and bulbs on these facades will depend on electricity to be supplied from the pole and various wires, instead of a smoky old showman's engine.

When I was painting here in March it was blowing a gale most days. The amusement arcade to the left of the one I show was actually running during the weekends. People carriers would arrive and deposits sets of kids and a granny to go inside to play the machines. Periodically, a mechanical voice would invite potential customers to: "Join in the flavour! Join in the flavour!" – meaning stuff more money into the machines.

Occasionally, people would come out with the usual rewards for winning, fluffy bunnies, and so on.

In season when all the amusement arcades are open, I doubt that I would have been able to get near enough to paint. At least I was spared the smell of frying hamburgers.

Exhibited: Royal Academy Summer Exhibition, 2000

THE STATION AT THORPE-LE-SOKEN

My mum was car-sick, so we went everywhere by train. When she took me to the seaside, it always seemed like ages that the train stopped at Thorpe, waiting for the connection from Clacton or Walton.

The picture tells it all. This super station is very much a Victorian relic, even the waiting rooms with the Great Eastern Railway GER cypher in their cast-iron mouldings look like old carriages.

I was taken on a conducted tour by Michael Rhodes, who works at the station and knows everything about its history. He told me that it was opened on July 18, 1866, originally just called Thorpe, to which -le-Soken was added in 1900. It was electrified in 1959. The signal box was built by Saxby and Farmer. Before it was electrified, it had a 70-lever signal frame, made by Mackenzie and Holland, of Worcester, in 1903.

One of the station's most famous tourists was Queen Mary, who used to alight at Thorpe to meet her chum Lady Byng, who lived nearby.

This is a painting that spanned the Millennium. I was working there on Christmas Day and Millennium Day.

Chas Debenham

THE GHOST AND THE GREYHOUND, *TIBENHAM*

I had seen Amanda in The Greyhound pub yard, telling her boxer puppy to "go do wee-wee" while I was stuck up in a field entrance painting. I was parked at a rather steep angle on the grass bank at the side of a track. Shortly after, her landlord husband John came over to check me out, disappointed that I was not painting the pub, to the left of my picture. Shortly after he left, Amanda hailed me from the middle of the road. "Coffee?" "With and with, thank you," I replied. Not only did I get coffee but a packet of Walker's crisps – that's a first.

John had been full of enthusiasm for his new wife and their new puppy. He had been in engineering, and they had only taken over a couple of weeks before.

I took the mug back to Amanda. "It's haunted, you know," she said, indicating the stable opposite, which I was painting. "About five years ago the previous owner had some work done, lowering the floor, and disturbed an evil spirit. When they tried to lead a horse in it went absolutely ballistic. The vet was asked to check the horse out, as it had always been well-behaved before. Other things began to go wrong then, in the pub, going missing or being moved." Next, the local vicar was called in, he spotted "the path of the spirit" between the stable and the pub, presumably, and after a swift exorcism things returned to normal, with the pub now only serving distilled spirits!

I painted this in the early summer of 2000. It was a pity that I had not been there five years before to witness the excitement. I was too late, too, to have a drink with James Stewart, the film star. The bar is full of photos relating to World War Two, American aircraft and crews that operated out of Tibenham airfield, now run as a flying club.

On my last painting day I met the ghost-buster, or ghost-releaser, whose work with the JCB had started it all. "Oh, that load of old tosh," was his comment on the incident but he would say that, wouldn't he?

Chas Debenham

ROBIN HOOD AND JUMBO, *COLCHESTER*

This picture was painted in the early 1980s and shows the Robin Hood pub and Colchester's Jumbo water tower. When you arrive by train at Colchester station, the first thing you see is Jumbo dominating the skyline.

It was originally a term of derision that became one of affection. The tower, built to improve Colchester's water supply, was officially opened in 1883. The rural dean and rector of St Mary's, concerned that the 130-foot tower would be built near his back door, criticised the scheme at the inquiry stage. He coined the nickname by which it was to become known, referring to the tower as "this monstrosity, this Jumbo". This referred to an event that had caused national uproar at that time, the selling of the famous elephant at London Zoo to the American circus proprietor, Phineas Barnum. An elephant weathervane was placed on top of the tower.

Originally Balkerne Tower, to give it its official name, had a huge gutter around the top. However, when it rained and the wind blew it would drench people below – a water tower in more than one sense! In 1908, work on the top of the tower included replacing the guttering. When the centenary of the tower occurred, I designed the booklet that commemorated Jumbo's history for Anglian Water, who took over ownership in 1974, and the celebration mug, limited to an edition of 100. The 1883 side of the mug shows the guys who built the tower and the bigwigs who opened it, the 1983 side showing the great and the good of modern Colchester.

The tower has changed hands once or twice since and is still causing controversy.

SATURDAY'S SIGHTS, *ALBION GROVE, COLCHESTER*

This is a painting I could no longer do, because it is an area where residents-only parking is now in force. You are very lucky if you can even manoeuvre through the parked cars here at any time of day. For someone like me it doesn't always solve the problem to go on foot, as with residential parking the cars are solid, so that everything gets obscured.

When I was painting this, the chappie in the blue shirt was always coming out and inquisitively, furtively looking, but never quite plucking up courage to come across and inspect what I was doing. He kept an eye on everything that was going on. It was only when such distractions as the two girls going by occurred that I ceased to be the subject of his attention.

This is one of those so-simple pictures that demand you just stand and observe to spot the oddities. For example, those are not white-painted bricks, but are actually tiles. It is only one house, but how about the variety of materials and shapes in that fence?

Exhibited: Royal Academy Summer Exhibition, 1984

WET CHRISTMAS, *COLCHESTER*

This was painted on a Christmas Day in the late 1980s, near Colchester North Station, with the town hall in the distance. The building on the right has had several changes of use, and is currently Tins Chinese Takeaway – I love that, Chinese takeaways in tins!

VICTORIAN FIREMEN'S COTTAGES, SUDBURY

This picture shows what a hassle it can be to work on the spot, as I do, but the subject was well worth it. I had to paint the cottages standing on a narrow path by the traffic lights with my back to a pub wall which vibrated to the throb of heavy electronic music. The traffic fumes were so bad that they made me cough like a 40-a-day man.

There are four cottages, built for Sudbury's Victorian fire brigade, with their remarkable imposing Saxon-style doorways. The station was situated on the right. Various subsequent tenants have left their mark on the cottages. Look at the repairs to the capital on the left and, more obviously, the alterations to the windows. What I found funny was that the owner of the cottage on the end, not shown in my picture, was clearly really annoyed because by the time he bought his house the council was insisting that he retain the original-style windows. Two other interesting things are hidden from view: the trapezium-shaped room plan – very inconvenient, one lady told me – and the end-of-garden ablutions block. Almost convenient.

Exhibited: Royal West of England Academy, 1999

CAFE, *GREAT TOTHAM, NEAR MALDON*

The map shows that there are two Great Tothams, about a mile apart, between Colchester and Maldon. My location was the one nearer Maldon. The picture was painted in 1999 from a little lay-by opposite. As I was working I would suddenly hear a clip-clop clip-cop and a shaggy skewbald pony would pass pulling a two-wheel trotting cart. The whole area is settled by what are known as travelling people, except that they are now static.

They are great characters. One of them came over, looked at the picture and asked: "Do you paint horses?" I replied: "Oh no, no." On reflection, I think that might have been foolish. Perhaps he would have asked me to paint his entire stud, payment in cash!

SCHOOL HOLIDAY, *WITHAM*

I would never have found this one from the car. This is the view that I saw from the train when it pulled into Witham station travelling up to Liverpool Street.

Out of the corner of my eye I saw this house where the whole corner window is built out at an angle, so I just had to return to look at it more closely. It had got to be a weekend painting, when the car park was near empty. To get the right angle I had to park in front of the pedestrian entrance, praying no official would make me move.

That window appeared on inspection to have been just a designer's whim. I could see no logic in it except it had been built for a retired railway guard.

Exhibited: Royal West of England Academy, 1993

THE GASOMETER, *BURY ST EDMUNDS*

I bought my Land Rover in Bury, and when it went in for its 14,000-mile service I made the drawing for this picture. I always enjoy walking around Bury, I feel quite evangelical about it. It won the Nation in Bloom 1999 contest, but I cannot paint flowers. What I could paint was this giant sponge-cake with icing on the top. I wanted to add candles, sing "Happy Birthday" and blow them out or is it up?

I started painting one sunny Sunday in the spring of 2000. The car park ticket machine leaves you uncertain whether or not you have to pay on Sundays. I had to work fairly swiftly, as leaves were beginning to show and I wanted the tree and lamp-post in a similar state. Luckily, I had few distractions. There were shoppers rattling their trolleys down the other end of the car park near Kwik Save, a few tourists debating whether or not they had to pay and a self-confessed frustrated artist who set up his camera behind me, taking my best view.

Later, I'm back in Bury for one of those recalls-to-garage for some part to be checked. With time to kill, I visit the local Record Office, where I'm given a folder of newspaper clippings about the gasworks. Among them is a photo of a Mr Churchill, a deep-sea diver in full gear, including copper helmet with portholes, working in a large well at the base of the gasometer in 1934, looking for gas leaks.

I realised that Mr Churchill and I had something in common. When I bought our house the plans showed a well, but not the actual location. We began discovering wells all over the place – brick ones, concrete ones but all turned out to be cesspits. A couple of years later Eilish, standing in the drive, asked: "Why is that the only square bit in the crazy paving?" We'd found the well. I located some Victorian well bricks to rebuild the top, and decided that the best way to do it was to sit on a plank astride the well and work round. After mixing mortar, I annoyingly dropped my trowel down the well, borrowed another, and dropped that in, too. With the mortar setting, I placed a long ladder down the well, donned swimming trunks and descended into very cold water, stirring up a cloud of silt. Troweless I climbed the ladder, found goggles, waited for the silt to settle and descended once more. The trowels decided that they want to stay with the muck and jetsam of centuries, so it was up the ladder again.

Bear in mind that from ground level the ladder, the well and I were invisible. So, imagine the horror of a family, out for a stroll along the bridle-way, mildly curious about work going on at the side of our house, when I emerge, begoggled and dripping, from the middle of the drive.

Not surprisingly, they made a very disorderly and hasty retreat.

Chas Debenham

Chas Debenham

TOM KEATING'S BILLET, *DEDHAM*

Many will remember Tom Keating, the restorer who achieved national fame by creating his own versions of Samuel Palmer, Rembrandt, Rubens and others and was able to fool the so-called experts.

I like to remember Tom from the days when a visit meant that I had to check we'd got at least a couple of bottles of brandy in. He would sit in our old red leather chair and by mid-evening he blended in perfectly, at which point he would retell – several versions in the same evening – that part of his life story dearest to him at that moment.

I loved his television series recreating masterpieces, which I still rate the best of its kind, although I told him they would have been better one minute shorter. On one of my visits to his studio, across the way from the billet, Tom was painting a version of Constable's *A Country Lane*, which shows a boy under trees drinking from a brook. It was a commission from a Sunday newspaper colour supplement to illustrate the effect of Dutch elm disease on the landscape. Tom was not working on canvas, though. He had bought a large reproduction and was simply painting over all the leaves.

He died in 1984, sixteen years before I completed this picture. I last saw him briefly at Liverpool Street station. "How are you?" I asked. "Still in the same damp old billet," he replied.

This view was not quite as I originally envisaged it. During the course of painting it, I had got quite chummy with Michael de Muscote-Morris, who owns the big house of which Tom Keating's billet is a satellite. I had to park in Mr de Muscote-Morris' drive, which meant that he had a slight difficulty getting his car past mine. When I turned up one day, he said: "Oh, I'll clear all this for you," referring to the foreground.

This he did, with a bulldozer removing half the foreground greenery. The tragedy of good intentions? No! Unintentionally, it helped much more than he thought, as now the scrape marks make it a simpler picture.

Initial drawing done with a brush in Payne's Grey on a hardboard panel primed with rabbit-skin size.

RA BITS, *SWAFFHAM*

The market was clearly in decline in Swaffham when I painted this in the summer of 2000. Whereas there had once been bustle behind The Greyhound in the centre of town, now there are no goats. Under the awning behind the propped-up caravan, all that is left are the cages that housed the rabbits and poultry, all piled up on top of one another in long rows, with a couple of RSPCA notices and a sign: "No straw in the pens. Thank you."

There is still a market of sorts here on Saturdays, The Greyhound's landlord told me. That accounted for the odd assortment of rickety tables herded up under the other awning, that still displays the letters ..RONE P ROB.RTS, with a sort of Braille image left by the fixings where letters have fallen off, leaving you to puzzle what it originally said.

Chas Debenham

PEASENHALL ART AND ANTIQUES GALLERY

The name alone would have been enough to make me paint this one, but there were other attractions. There is the security notice at the side, though I never saw the guardian, then there were the colours. As I developed the painting I discovered the pattern made by the angle of the roof tiles and the bricked-up door on the left, plus the marvellous propped-up signs – there's one on the right side as well: "ANTIQUES OPEN" written in black felt-tip on sheets of old cardboard.

This is an architectural classic. The shop front built over the small front garden. In its previous life the shop's fascia proudly stated "Draper G HORNER Grocer". The dog would have been guarding the "Corn and Flour Merchants" and the buildings would have cast their shadow on what was then The Angel pub.

Mike Wickins had been running the gallery and restoring paintings for 26 years by the time I painted it in 2000. Before that, he had played centre-forward for Chelsea. When I said I wanted to paint the gallery with the door open he agreed (it was mid-winter).

I painted this parked under the trees opposite, in a large, very deep puddle. This fortunately put off most other would-be parkers, so that I could regain my position on each visit. Getting an unobstructed view was another question. Besides waiting for the gallery's customers and other temporary parkers to shift, cars parked permanently were more of a problem. The lady who worked in the butcher's up the road was happy to reposition her Citroën, though the guys on the counter were a little curious when I asked.

PEASENHALL ART & ANTIQUES GALLERY

BEWARE
DOG

Chas Debenham

FOGGY SUNDAY, *GREAT BENTLEY*

When I look out of my window and find that it is foggy, I know that if I am going to paint that day I have only got one shot at it. Not knowing how long the conditions are going to last, it has got to be a quick sketch, done close to home.

That was the case one Sunday in January 1997, when I chose to paint the good solid shape of the Wesleyan Chapel on Great Bentley's green, with its roof which kept blurring into the self-coloured mist. As I worked I saw a light go on, then watched a congregation of three car loads and one or two brave souls turn up on foot. I had better get the cars recorded before they disappeared.

Now and again I heard the sound of hymns. Later, I learned that it was Mrs Fookes at the organ. She had "filled in" in the 1960s and is a fixture now. Her daughter says: "Mum, you're jazzing up the hymns too much!" The Reverend Frazer J Hawkes says: "Joan, you're more of a pianist." She certainly helped brighten up my foggy Sunday.

DAY TRIPPERS, *GREAT BENTLEY STATION*

When I saw this bridge at Bentley, half way between Colchester and Clacton, it reminded me of my toy train set. Here, they have clearly heightened the bridge to allow the electricity lines to pass beneath it.

I painted this in 1994 from the car park of the village hall, a modern one which always has things going on in it. Each time I arrived hoping that my chosen space would be free. It is a detailed subject, so it would have taken anything up to 15 sittings, and being the summer this would have meant longer hours.

One day when I turned up the entire car park was full. A fun run was being organised from the hall. The runners were being shunted off in sections: ladies first, then the kids, then the serious runners, and so on. As well as runners and organisers, there were people drifting in to see them off and welcome them back again. The police parted the waves for me, and there I was painting perched among a load of amateur athletes.

Exhibited: Royal West of England Academy, 1994

Chas Debenham

FRIARS STREET, *SUDBURY*

This is the end of an imposing terrace. It was another of those narrow-pavement jobs, although the easel did fit partly into a recess in the house at the side. This solved the pram-passing problem, but brought me into the droppings zone, not only dogs but birds, too, as it was just under the eaves. The picture was completed in the spring of 1999, and fortunately the weather held for days.

I was offered several versions of my painting location's history while I was there. "It was a school." "I think it used to be a" and so on. Most locals were lacking the local Suffolk accent, and probably local knowledge. None seemed to think of the buildings just as lovely dwellings. Speculation was probably more interesting than fact. I bet the place next door had some good stories to tell, too.

I have a long relationship with Sudbury, my aunts and uncles all having lived or worked there. My cousin Pam worked in Steed and Steed's solicitors office in Gainsborough Street, a short distance from the house where Thomas Gainsborough was born, which is now a really excellent small museum.

I was doing a pen and wash drawing of Market Hill one winter, perched under Gainsborough's statue. I don't know which one of us was the coldest. It was as I sat there, frozen, that a drunk, ejected from the Black Boy pub, staggered over to me, asking: "Do you know Ruskin?"

Chas Debenham

REDUNDANT WATER TOWER, *MANNINGTREE*

The bridge with the bright black and yellow markings on it carries the main railway line from Colchester to Ipswich and Norwich. If you are going on to Harwich, the line splits here. The road divides, too, to enable big vehicles such as heavy lorries to continue, as they would not be able to get under the bridge. It is one of those places where there is a priority for traffic from the other side.

If it is wet, going under the bridge can be a bit exciting. I painted this in the mid-1990s. By that time, of course, the water tower which served the steam trains was long redundant.

Exhibited: Royal West of England Academy, 2000

ARTILLERY FOLLEY, *COLCHESTER*

This was painted near the centre of Colchester. The Folley – the spelling is local – is really a barracks wall running the entire length on the south side, and on the north side there are the backs of houses.

This picture illustrates some of the dangers of standing in the street painting. I had noticed that the grass growing against the wall was littered with drug users' needles, indicating that it was a place for shooting up in the evenings.

When I painted this in the mid-1990s a couple of unsettling incidents occurred. First, I was approached from the back by a young man, quite small, sporting a baseball bat, wearing a red bandanna round his head, his clothing professionally ripped to emphasise his image and masculinity. The ensuing conversation was rather more an inquiry as to whether I had got any cash than anything else. I never carry money with me, so he would have been out of luck. He eventually departed and I was quite relieved.

The second incident occurred when a chappie riding a bike stopped at the barrier you can see at the bottom of the picture and came up the steps with it, then tore off down the Folley. A few minutes later a teenage boy appeared and asked: "Have you seen anyone riding a blue mountain bike?" Clearly, the first man had stolen it from down the road. I told the owner what I had seen, and he went off to the police station nearby. I described the chappie on the bike to the police. They knew exactly who he was and where he lived, but explained that by the time they got to him he would have sold it.

Chas Debenham

REG WILLIAMS, *EDWARDSTONE*

Reg had his ninetieth birthday while I was painting this, the second view of his historic loo, in 1997. The propped-up apple tree was, like him, on its "last legs" – his joke. The garden, with its orderly rows of vegetables and neat groups of flowers, was always well tended, unlike the house, shabby and run-down.

Reg would appear shortly after I arrived. He would dig and re-dig the same patch, staying just within commentary range, but you could not have wished for a better model. He had a very dry wit and beautiful gravelly accent. Reg was the son of a tenant farmer and had worked on the land at Groton Hall, in the next village.

He would try to sell you anything. He'd show you things like wartime matchbox covers, saying: "Is that worth anything? It's got Churchill and Roosevelt on." But he always gave me some vegetables after a small ceremony of digging them up and quiz on propagation. This all started after he said that I was a "townee", and probably had a pocket handkerchief for a garden. When I told him that I had an acre-plus on him, he replied: "Well, that puts me in my place", but recovered the advantage when I said that my wife did all the work and could not grow carrots, his speciality.

I painted this standing by the side of Reg's old garage-cum-pigsty. Both car and pigs had long since gone. The tin bath was one of many, all pressed into service as water-butts. The privy, with a top vent, like the tin baths had been replaced by a modern bathroom, which filled the space between it and the cottage. The coal store, the other white door, seemed to have extended into the lean-to.

I have painted six different views of these cottages at School Green. Shortly after I finished this and two other views, with his neighbour Mrs Green, Reg went into hospital and died later in a nursing home.

NO. 18, BEVERLEY ROAD, *COLCHESTER*

In the same year I painted three pictures in Beverley Road within 50 feet of one another. They all ended up within a few feet of each other hanging in the Academy. It is often the case that when I start one painting I begin to think: "Well, why don't I paint that bit over there?", and so on.

The old boy leaning on the wall was actually the road-sweeper, but he insisted on being in the picture. So I said: "Don't stand here," with his cart, "but there." And with that he moved up into the drive.

This diamond-decorated brickwork is highly characteristic of the area. Look at the chimneys, turned around so that they, too, are diamonds.

Exhibited: Royal Academy Summer Exhibition, 1982

FAITH, HOPE AND CHARITY, *WORTHAM LONG GREEN*

I came upon this splendid subject by chance. I had started out by car to visit the Norfolk Ploughing Championships, but missed the A140 turning and ended up near Bury St Edmunds. It was while taking the A143 to get back on course that I found Wortham's magnificent school gate. The following week I returned by a more direct route to paint the scene from the closed-up bit of the old main road.

The words Faith, Hope and Charity are now barely visible in the eroded sandstone blocks over the arches. I think it is an old bike shed that you can see through the first arch. Boys and girls must have felt important and rather special as they filed through their own arch, although I suspect not as important as those who passed through the bigger central arch.

On one of my visits, I was approached by a lady who was making a nostalgic return. She and her husband had driven from south London to see the school which she had attended as an evacuee during the Second World War. Memories of sirens and gas mask drills were exchanged and comments on the Portakabin additional classrooms.

Exhibited: Royal West of England Academy, 1997

THE VILLAGE HALL, *BRENT ELEIGH*

Although it is now the village hall, the bell told me that it used to be the village school. One winter weekend when I was there a squad of young men arrived in a van, ladders were put up against the wall and there was a lot of grumbling and blue language. It turned out that they were young offenders, doing community service on a Saturday, probably instead of causing mayhem at a local football match. In the end, I think they did more harm than good to the building they were supposed to be improving.

The young lady sorting through her change for a phone call was picked up 20 minutes later by a taxi.

Exhibited: Royal West of England Academy, 1990

THE GAZEBO, *BURNHAM MARKET*

When a building is as distinctive as this, it is unusual if it has not been done before. In 1967, Hew Purchas painted it for a National Savings poster, in December 1994 Andrew Dodds drew it for the *Eastern Daily Press* and doubtless other artists have had a go. After the best part of a day seeking subjects and looking at endless cloned flint buildings, I alighted on The Gazebo. I was fascinated by its roof, peering over the alley by the side of the Post Office. It is deceptive, the painted image not being able to convey all the peculiarities of its construction, such as the flat roof in front and ridged roof at the back.

The owners, Roy and Cindy Stimpson, are kindred spirits. Coffee and house history, accompanied by piles of deeds and wills relating to their property, are served simultaneously. As we sit on the terrace, I learn that The Gazebo was built in 1760, when it was known as The Look-Out. It seems that the builder wanted to be able to scan the sea, so there were trap-doors in the roof making this possible. From the cellars there was a network of tunnels, some of which later caved in. Was all this to spot revenue cutters or friendly French free-traders? The Gazebo entered the Stimpson family in 1911, when Roy's grandfather, Frederick, moved from Thorpe to open the village Post Office. After the First World War, part of the shop served as the Labour Exchange. The Stimpsons ran the Post Office until 1977.

Roy's tale of how his dad destroyed the outside loo is topped by Cindy's loo story. She had spotted a picture in a charity auction and just had to have it. "Through the arch was the row of houses where my aunt lived with the corresponding row of loos just round the corner. On a cold winter's night, torch and toilet paper in hand, you would arrive at your loo to find it occupied, the pub was just down the street. 'Can't you hang on a minute? Can't you go next door? Well, you didn't think I could hang on till I got home!'"

Meanwhile, while we chat, a local builder, Jimmy, has been mending the Post Office roof. Mid-afternoon, mug in hand, he comes across to inspect my progress. His own has been hampered, as his "help" has let him down. "He wanted £11.50 an hour, more than I bloody get." By Sunday morning Jimmy has cheered up a bit, having got some help. I remark on his Sunday-best working attire. "'Sno good turning up in a tweed jacket," he replies. "This" — his paint-grimed clothes — "tells them what I do, and they can afford me."

He asks me how I get jobs. Do I have a card? He gave me his own leaflet. He told me that he lived in Burnham Thorpe, birthplace of Admiral Lord Nelson. Later, I took a good look at Jimmy's flyer. Almost incredibly, his full name was James Hamilton, living at No. 2 Nelson's Close. . . .

Chris Debenham

UNDER THE BRIDGE OVER THE YARE, *NEAR NORWICH*

This bridge, like its concrete counterpart the Hayward Gallery in London, also has a fine collection of original works, mainly life studies in the spray-can medium. It too has a river view, day-captains at the wheel of large motor boats, their ladies dangling bare legs over the pointy bit.

MR HARDWICK'S DAIRY, *RAWSTORN ROAD, COLCHESTER*

It was only after I had started drawing the narrow passage-way that Mr Hardwick's image came back to me: flat cap, funny moustache and apron, pushing his hand-cart, a milk churn on wheels. He set out from his dairy twice a day, traipsing around filling the local jugs with half and pint measures. My mum got her milk from the Co-op, horse-drawn.

As I was painting, a young woman brought me much-appreciated mugs of coffee from across the road. She never knew that a dairy had existed in the back yard of her neighbour, commenting: "You must have done a lot of research." Then I told her that it had been in the tin hall opposite her, now used as a day care centre, that in my youth I had spent many hours hurling myself at a vaulting horse. Practising for our local display team, village fêtes a speciality. (Half the team kitted out in whites on loan from Arthur Clutten's dad's fish shop.)

A remarkable event occurred during my final struggles with this picture. I was not satisfied with the initial painting of the foreground, which I had decided must be changed, so I spent a morning taking out the road and the pavement. It was a weekday, when I knew the road would be mainly clear because it was residents-only parking, so I shot back, put up my easel and started to paint. As I was working, a small contractor's open-backed van came up the hill and pulled in just past me. A guy climbed out and said: "Just the man! Just the man! — I've got something for you."

Could he be speaking to me, I wondered? He repeated: "Just the man! — I've been looking for you." He returned to the van and came back with a mahlstick, probably Victorian, beautifully covered in tooled leather. It's the device that steadies your hand when you are working on a picture, preventing you touching wet paint. Handing it to me, he said: "I took it out of a skip a couple of weeks ago, and I thought, 'Pity to throw that away'." And with that, off he went. No attempt to sell it, or to make unnecessary conversation, and I still don't know who he was. It restored my faith in human nature.

This shows day two of work, the start of painting in colour after the initial drawing. You can see where Mr Hardwick's cart went, up the right half of the path, down which a dividing fence extended.

BLACK AND WHITE IN WET, *WALTON*

This was painted concurrently with the other Walton-on-the-Naze picture, *Out of Season, Walton*, at the end of the 1990s. I would motor down with both pictures. If the day was wet I painted this one, if fine I would move about 100 metres to work on the other one.

This view cries out to be painted, it's divinely simple – it's a gem. When I first saw this building it was in sunshine, but then when I arrived to start painting the sky clouded over and it chucked it down, really highlighting the scene. With the black sky everything stood out, so much clearer.

Look at the details on the buildings: for example, the little spiky ridge tiles with some bits missing, the fretted pattern in the eaves and that beautiful bargeboard. See the contrast of the original windows in the right-hand block and the centre. When you move across to the left-hand side they have replaced the windows with smaller ones, and you can see a line where the original windows were.

One Sunday, this couple arrived, doubling up on the title. They were clearly a unit, the little lady pulling her trolley, the guy built just like the building.

Exhibited: South West Academy, 2000

DOWNPOUR IN THETFORD

Mid-May to mid-June was pretty wet. The weekends were the only time I could paint this subject. It was the only time there was a space just by the entrance to the lorry park where I could just squeeze in, surrounded by Chas Morris Transport, CW Tanker Services, Daily Fresh Logistics and Thetford Transport Training.

London Road crosses Bury Road here, the traffic lights ensuring that my view was regularly obscured by a succession of towed tilts and tautliners, tankers, tour coaches, container lorries and spray. What attracted me was the fascinating difference in wall textures in this row of houses. Apart from the flint update at the end, the rest is made up of a variety of different layers of material, all of which, I suspect, periodically fell off the back of someone's cart a century or so ago.

Chas Debenham

MRS GREEN, *WATERING, EDWARDSTONE*

I painted several views of these two cottages over the winter of 1997, moving my easel round from one side to the other. If it wasn't freezing it was misty. I protected myself with thick boots, two pairs of socks and layers and layers of clothes, resembling an East Anglian Compo, the character in the television series *Last of the Summer Wine*, or Michelin Man.

I got to know Mrs Green and her neighbour Reg Williams, very well, although they "didn't get on". Reg was taken into hospital as I was painting this picture, and died shortly after the series was completed.

Originally, I was attracted to the front of these beautiful Victorian cottages, then I realised that they were more interesting around the back because of the outbuildings. The dustbin, featured in another picture, had become a compost bin, as the cottages had been provided by the council with wheelie-bins. Other examples of modernisation are Mrs Green's oil tank and plastic flower-pot. Whereas Reg's garden was perfect and his house was a bit of a shambles, Mrs Green's house and garden, which she did herself, were both immaculate.

THE BRIDGE AT BURES HAMLET

A scene painted at the approaches to Bures station in the early '90s that gives a misleading air of tranquillity. I chose to ignore the traffic as did the old boy with the bicycle, around whose bulk the many cars had to manoeuvre as he took up position in the middle of the road. He would appear on a regular basis, from his allotment on the other side of the bridge. Thus situated, he would hold a conversation with me at my easel, with anyone else on the pavement or with Dulcie, shown at the door of the cottage that used to be the local police station until the 1950s. His was literally a push-bike, a means of support, as he never actually rode it.

I was the recipient of many cups of coffee from ladies with rival stories as I painted this. One concerned the lady who had bought the house next door for her son when he got married. He returned from his honeymoon to find she had knocked a doorway through the first-floor landings, so she could keep an eye on him and his new bride — all good neighbourly fun.

Chas Debenham

HOLLS, VETERINARY SHOEING FORGE, *NEW BUCKENHAM*

High summer 2000, and I take up my strategic position on the elevated part of the green at New Buckenham. By placing myself between the phone box and the waste bin, I am under the cover of trees and command the best view: that little bit of space between the two buildings, the patterns pivoting around the centred window.

Then they struck! Thousands (well hundreds) of thunder flies. Suddenly, I am doing my impression of tennis ace John McEnroe at Wimbledon to keep them off as they swarm over me and the picture, making it a living tableau.

Following visits went better, with no flies and only one chap using the bin. One day, when it is past 3pm and I am done with painting, I try to decipher the name on the end of the building in my picture. I remain mystified, so knock on the door of the house by the side of the forge. Answering it, Stephanie said that she could not remember. "Come in. I'll ask my husband," but when she came back: "No. He's fast asleep." She looked out of the window, to the King's Head, at the far side of the green. "Ask them. They'll know." I crossed the green, as I approached I'm reminded of years ago when I had cartilage trouble and couldn't keep balance when mounting kerbs. One of the chaps seemed to have the same problem. "When the light's right, you can see it easily: H O L L S," he says. There are still some of them around. It's over 40 years since the forge was working." "Nearer 50," comments the other.

Finishing touches day arrives, and I set up my easel accompanied by rumblings of thunder. As I did so, cyclists assemble under the Market Cross. They filter past in their colourful, trendy, clingy kit, and space wars helmets, pedalling in low gear. Then I got a clue to their advanced ages from their rather more upright, sturdy black machines – the Saga Cycling Club, perhaps?

I work on. Kids are now on holiday and visit me in small swarms, some on foot, followed by mounted support groups. One angelic little girl is always last. She'd hurt her foot sliding down a haystack. Now I answer the questions. I am struck by their real interest and how polite they all are as they monitor my progress during the day.

Chas Debenham

AUGUST XMAS, *WIVENHOE*

In a picturesque place like Wivenhoe, you cannot get away from what I term pick 'n' mix recommendations from passers-by about the best view to paint. "There's a better ... a lovely ... a beautiful ... on the front ... just round the corner," and so on: advice I got every day I was working there.

I found this corner far more interesting. Look at that reverse-stepped pyramid on the corner of the building, the simple pattern of signs and windows, the low-and high-pitched roofs and the fading-tinsel humour of the chap putting out his rubbish and you might pun: bags of interest. I call this August Xmas, for it was painted in the hot summer of 1999. The Christmas decorations had been up so long that they had faded, but they still drew an awful lot of comment.

THE RED HOUSE, *WIVENHOE*

Originally this started life as an 8"×10", but I never really got the right side right, so I cut it off. I was against the church tower to paint this one. I was also against the vicar, who wanted to charge me for the privilege.

The grey oblong behind the railings to the left of the gate is the back of the BT phone box in the picture opposite.

Chas Debenham

MR VINCENT'S WORKSHOP, *LAXFIELD*

This gravity-defying structure, great fun for the artist, was itself painted, I suspect, with what was left over in the pots from various jobs. The rusting iron defences and the gate look as if they have been rescued from a scrapyard and fit in perfectly with the twisted old fruit tree.

I can well imagine Mr Vincent. One summer holiday, in my early teens, I provided the locomotive power for a jobbing builder's hand-cart, amply loaded with sand, cement, tools and a ladder. I gained my first, invaluable knowledge of what is now known as DIY, but remember the blisters most.

The picture was painted late in 1999. Around the fourth sitting I had a chat with the present owner, Mike Devereau, who lives in a house to the left of the workshop. He took me on a grand tour of the building. In contrast to the external look the inside was undergoing a major refit, to convert it into a studio for his artist wife Sarah.

While I was painting the picture I revisited one of the local pubs, The King's Head, known as The Lower House, thatched, unique and unchanged since I was last there with a friend 10 years before. Only the cast was different. On my first visit we had hardly sat down before we were being thoroughly interrogated by the regulars, then after swapping lifestyles, rounds were exchanged, time passed, more rounds and so on. Then something happened that still makes me smile.

Two of these chaps, who all seemed to work on the land, had a mate who must have been doing a bit of hedging and ditching and had got a blackthorn in his thumb, covered by a grubby bandage. Seems it had been in a long time, and that he was afraid to see a doctor. More rounds brought more courage and the decision that an immediate operation was required. One man, who had a strong Dutch accent, sharpened his pruning knife, the patient was laid over the pine table, and there was an atmosphere of tension. Suddenly, the landlady said: "Hold on!", disappeared and came back with a bottle containing about three fingers of whisky left in it. "That's not enough," complained the surgeon. "It's all I've bloody well got," said the landlady. I think that the surgeon, the patient and thumb got a finger each, but I never found out if the patient recovered.

Chs Debenham

RESIDENTIAL DEVELOPMENT OPPORTUNITY, *BROCKDISH*

I picked up my old mate Andrew Dodds, who does a weekly drawing for the *Eastern Daily Press*. "Take me to the parts of Norfolk other artists never reach, or want to go," I said.

We turned right, off the A140. Going through Brockdish, I saw this view of a disused garage with a For Sale sign: "Residential Development Opportunity". All over Norfolk you see developments, little groups of builders standing around pallet-loads of pink bricks done up in plastic, tarting up the place.

Andrew is not sure that he can find enough interest in Brockdish, so we drive on, seeking something that will appeal to us both. Like a talking Pevsner guide, Andrew points out attractions before we get to them: "Old Alfred Munnings came from over there", we pass The Lord Nelson, the roads get narrower, the scenery really good for an artist like him. But today it's my car, and I want buildings.

Coincidentally, as we turn a corner I see a piebald pony, which kicks up its hooves, plunges along the verge, reaches the end of its tether and careers back alongside us. It belongs with a little group of those old Romany-style, round-roofed caravans, accompanied by more horses, even more dogs, kids, washing, smoke and clutter. Was this The Alfred Munnings Re-enactment Society? Finding nothing suitable

for us both, we return to Brockdish and the Residential Development Opportunity which had first appealed to me, back past The Lord Nelson. Even that was being redeveloped.

I set up the easel in front of the garage. I start to paint, measuring the distances in the correct manner – arm fully extended, thumb notching up the scale on the brush handle, firmly focused, *one eye closed*.

It was not the best idea to finish this painting on a Saturday. Half-a-dozen of the local lads had piled up pallets on the garage forecourt, were using a board as a ramp, getting up speed in the road to perfect cycle-jumping techniques. This was interspersed with interludes of football and playing with the forecourt hose. Just what I needed – a wet surface and performing kids.

Finally, they found a more participative audience up the road, outside the Post Office, two young mums having to defend their young. "I'll tell your f---ing mum!" More quick cycle manoeuvring, "I'll get the f---ing police!", and so on. Up there, it's all action, but I am left in peace.

Exhibited: Royal West of England Academy, 2000

Chas Debenham

Chas Debenham

ALDERFORD MEWS, *SIBLE HEDINGHAM*

It was a long time since I had been back in Hedingham. It was not long before the occupant of this amusing little house came out with her little dog and started to do some intensive gardening while looking over her shoulder, clearly keen to know what I was doing. Eventually, she did come over, remarking: "I've got a picture of my house done by Leonard Squirrell." Up the steep grass bank and into the house we went to see it. There was the Squirrell, triumphantly displayed with a sort of "Follow that, mate," quality. "Oh, it's one of those railway pictures," I remarked. It took me back to my childhood when you sat in the railway carriage compartment facing two long, narrow pictures of places, normally seaside resorts, designed to make you select next year's holiday destination.

This lady's Squirrell showed the whole of the Sible Hedingham street, but the scene had slightly changed. In the days when Leonard had painted his picture her house was part of the one next door, with a great central chimney, now taken out. It was logical that the railway company commissioned Squirrell. He was an Ipswich-born painter and etcher, notable for landscapes and architectural views, well represented in national collections. As well as being a masterly etcher, he was a fluent watercolourist, inspired by John Sell Cotman.

SUNDAY JOBS, *HALSTEAD*

There were many features which attracted me to this view, the odd angles, the lovely curve on the wall by the dog, the bargeboards on the house on the left and on the opposite house the zig-zag bricklaying. I thought: this is great!

The problem was where to site the easel, as this is a very narrow, winding road, on a steep hill. The pavement is less than three feet wide. So I asked the people who owned the house at my back if I could paint from their small front garden. My elevated position above the road, and you can see how deep that is, hid me from pedestrians passing underneath who unwittingly shared their gossip with me.

The guy opposite with his paint pot seemed to have come out to be in the picture, so I obliged. You get a lot of that. The trouble is that most people make their appearance after you have completed the composition. Young lads, especially, pose momentarily. You think, well, if you had appeared three weeks ago, and stayed there like the dog, you would have been in, mate.

Exhibited: Royal Academy Summer Exhibition, 1990

BREWER'S ARMS, *COLCHESTER*

I painted this picture of The Brewer's Arms in the 1960s. The scene has altered a bit since then. On the left the street is now pedestrianised, with car parking instead of houses at the other end. This is a head-on picture painted from the pavement. Near where I put my easel there used to be a newspaper office, the starting point for one of the funniest stories I was ever told.

It seems that at one time the advertising manager of the newspaper, who modelled himself on reporters in American films, had adopted a trenchcoat and a jaunty trilby hat, only lacking the small card tucked in the band announcing: "Press." Leaving his office one morning to sell a six-inch-double ad, he decided to stop off at The Brewer's Arms where he joined a group of men at the bar surrounding a lone woman, rounds being exchanged in a bid for her favours. Our man could out-drink anybody, so when he was the last man standing, obviously thinking his luck was in, he suggested going home with her for a cup of coffee.

The woman agreed, but said that first she must hand in a suitcase to the police station, which was then at the end of the street on the left. Being a gentleman he offered to carry it, but on bending down found that he could hardly lift it. Even so, he staggered with it to the police station.

There, she explained that she ran a lodging-house and that a lodger had left the suitcase and had disappeared. The sergeant on the desk suggested that they pass it over, where it was found to be locked.

However, he managed to open it (the lid obscuring the contents from our friends), closed it and asked our man: "Are you with this lady?" He, of course, replied: "Yes", so the sergeant said: "Would you mind both remaining here for a moment, while I get my inspector."

He duly arrived, the lid was lifted and closed again, whereupon the inspector asked them to confirm that they were together, and did they know what was in the case? No! They were then shown the contents, and asked to identify themselves. He explained his connection with the local paper. Could he verify it? "Yes, ring my editor." A description was given, identity was confirmed, and an irate editor could be heard asking why the advertising man was not on newspaper business, demanding his immediate return.

After the police said that they could go, the newspaper rep, who was not one to give up easily, headed off with the lodging-house lady for his cup of coffee. Indoors, she said that she would pop the kettle on. While she was doing so our friend crept up behind her. She – realising his intentions – turned round, picking up a saucepan full of baked beans, wedged it firmly over his head and threw him into the street, face dripping in tomato sauce. While hammering on the door, presumably to return the pan, our friend is spotted by a passing patrol car, is asked to explain the situation and identify himself and replies, "Ask your sergeant, he knows me. I was in the station only 10 minutes ago." "Oh, yes, we know him," the sergeant confirmed. "He's the chap who was in here earlier with a suitcase full of explosives!"

OUT OF SEASON, *WALTON*

Walton-on-the-Naze is a seaside town between Harwich and Clacton. It is one of those quiet resorts of which you have fond childhood memories, with mum taking you on the half-an-hour trip from Colchester on the steam train.

The picture shows the back of a lovely curved terrace of boarding houses. The rather run-down state of the buildings in the late 1990s is indicated by the one on the left.

The out-of-season time is shown by the lack of cars in the car park. Just on my left as I painted this were a number of recycling bins. Periodically, I would hear a great clank as people dropped in their bottles. There were also bins for clothing and newspapers. There was a predator who must have had a perch somewhere nearby, because immediately after someone put clothes in the appropriate bin he suddenly appeared, reaching in so far that his whole arm disappeared until he could pull out a garment to see if it was any good. This ritual extended to the other bins. He was keen to see if there were any dregs left in the bottles. Some newspapers and magazines were very highly prized.

This is very much a retirement place. I was amazed how often I would hear the low purr of an electric-powered invalid vehicle, crossing the car park.

When I priced this picture, it had to reflect the parking charges (all the receipts are stuck to the back of the picture). If the weather continued good for painting I had to keep feeding the meter, because I did not want to pay for time that I could not work there. It became a joke between me and the parking attendant that he had to cross the entire town from another car park just to go through the ritual of checking that I had a valid ticket.

Chas Debenham

AFTER SCHOOL, *ST JOHN'S GREEN, COLCHESTER*

Every artist paints at least one picture he or she never really wants to sell. This one is mine, as until the age of 11 this was my school. Memories include umpteen renderings of *Ten Green Bottles*, and being told off for stopping and trying to remove one of the Second World War incendiary bomb fins from the asphalt in the school playground, on the way to another rendition.

Exhibited: Royal West of England Academy, 1987

Chas Debenham

THE OLD SCHOOL, *OLD BUCKENHAM*

This location was deceptively tranquil when I parked one Tuesday after the May 2000 bank-holiday. It was not until I heard kids' voices behind me that I realised I was next to a play area, where three young ladies were playing a guessing game, shredding the characters of their friends and foes. "I'm small and thin..." "I'm all dressed in..." "I wear pongy perfume..." And so on, accompanied by lots of laughter, which drifted in through my open side window.

Meanwhile, my first and most important lines are going in. I'm fully focused.

A resident, Olive Shickle, explained to me that my subject had been the old school. "There wasn't a proper playground, so the kids played on the green." It is the church hall now, and Olive keeps the keys. She had a book which gave the history. "Mr Hart and his wife were the last teachers, living in the house built onto the side of the school, which closed in Easter, 1938."

I returned on Saturday to start colouring in. I love that phrase, with its memories of Sunday School. Something had been added to the scene, "*OLD BUCKENHAM SHOTOKAN KARATE CLUB, EVERY FRIDAY NIGHT, FRIENDLY BUT FIRM TUITION.*" painted (not by a sign-writer) in black on a wooden board leant against the wall of the churchyard.

Now, I face a big decision. Do I keep the sky uninterrupted, or put the oak tree branches in? The sky is a bit bland, so go for it and put the branches in!

The scene remains deceptively tranquil. About lunchtime, when my mind was still sorting out the oak tree, a small, reddish car parked in front of the karate notice. It is the hottest day of the year so far, so I have all the windows down. Voices from the other car come drifting in... One is funny and shrill, just like Mister Punch but female, with a whining male response. The little reddish car rocks slightly and as the volume increases I realise why, it is a fully-fledged row with the choicest language.

I could not see the contestants behind the head rests. Finally, the shrill voice announces: "We might as well go - - - - - 'oom, then!" The car starts up, turns a half circle, the driver sees me for the first time, and his mouth drops a little lower. Then Punching Judy unleashes a wicked right-cross to his jaw, the door opens, his safety belt holds and they are gone, "back - - - - - 'oom".

Both looked well past retirement. I think they just came on the wrong day.

Chas Debenham

SUNDAY NEWSPAPERS, *CAVENDISH*

Although I painted this picture on weekdays as well as Sundays, it got its title because on Sundays, directly the last newspaper was sold, the owner shut up the shop. I was there over several weeks in 1986. About half way through, I had a knock on the car window, and a lady, tiny and almost invisible from where I sat, asked: "Would you like coffee?" I said that would be splendid, so off she trotted. A little later there was a knock on the window, and there she was this time with the coffee – a cup on a silver tray, with a silver pot and biscuits. I could hardly believe it. She indicated where I was to return the tray, which I did, and it was only later that I learned she was Sue Ryder, who founded the Sue Ryder Foundation and its chain of charity shops.

Exhibited: Royal Academy Summer Exhibition, 1986

HARLEQUIN HOUSE, *STOWMARKET*

I came whipping round the corner in my car and thought: "That's fine, an excellent subject." It was winter, so I needed to work from inside the car, but there seemed nowhere to park. That was until I noticed that they were demolishing the house in the left-hand corner of the picture. It took several tries, but eventually I got into position, among the rubble way above the pavement where I normally would have been. The final picture must have taken about ten sessions in that awkward position. What had attracted me was the pattern in the bricks, and the bricked-up window on the right. It is the only brick pattern of that type that I have ever seen.

Exhibited: Royal Academy Summer Exhibition, 1989

CHANDLER'S HARDWARE, *BILDESTON*

Bildeston is a pleasant village, with old weavers' cottages and a church out in the fields. This had to be a Sunday painting, as it was the only day that I stood a chance of getting the spot vacant in the car park. Sunday painting meant that I was not there during weekday opening, when Chandler's put all their clutter outside: loads of ladders that made it look as if they were under a medieval siege, drums of this and that, brooms, barrows – the kitchen sink. It has all gone now, the character, but not the building.

I painted this in the early 1990s. You didn't need the sign to tell you they sold paraffin, as the fragrance lasted easily through Sunday.

Chas Debenham

BEACH HUTS, *WEST MERSEA*

I completed this in the winter of 1999. It was pretty blowy, and squalls kept coming in up the River Blackwater.

My visits coincided with the hut refurbishing programme. Cars would arrive, ladies would descend with their dogs, husbands unloading boots full of tools and B&Q bags. Some of the dogs would be desperate or just eager to record their arrival, their mistresses looking up and down the road hoping they were unobserved.

Chas Debenham

WILBY & SONS, *DICKLEBURGH*

Martin and Jenny will probably be the last in the line of Wilbys to run this family butcher's. T Wilby & Sons was established in 1888 by a great-great-grandfather, moving to the present site in 1890. Judging from photographic evidence pinned up in the little room at the side of the shop, little seems to have changed since then.

I am painting this in the summer of 2000, over the road in the entrance to a pub's car park. Each time a lorry passes, usually well over the speed limit, a vacuum sucks up a cloud of dust from behind me, adding more texture to the wet paint. Other than that, it is a really good position, protected from the sun. I am inspected by several dogs walking their owners, having a chat with a much-tattooed and pierced young man walking his poodle and his mum's Neapolitan mastiff.

As well as acting as a sunshade, the pub also serves as a watering and dewatering hole. Inside, I meet Golly Barrett, Jenny's uncle, who rides a bright pink ladies' mountain bike, the subject of much wit. Golly and I share a common dress sense. He was winding up the landlord, and looking at me, on the subject of haircuts, "more left on the floor", and so on.

The barber's shop is at the centre of the row of buildings in a courtyard at the side of the butcher's, and on the end is the old slaughter-house, last used over 50 years ago. The hooks from the roof beams still have the tin collars on them that prevented rats from gnawing the carcasses. I was told that when the pigs squealed it upset the kids in the school nearby.

MILL HILL, *SHIMPLING*

These houses might well have been built as part of an estate, as you see the same design cropping up around here. Now they are showing signs of individual ownership.

It was the simplicity of the houses that initially drew me to them. I liked the shape over the windows echoed in the porch design. Look at the disintegrating old iron fence held together with rust.

The title tells you that this is a high spot, subject to a lot of wind. Note the acid green windbreak in the neighbour's garden. I painted the picture in the mid-1990s in the early spring, cocooned and unapproachable in my car.

Exhibited: Royal West of England Academy, 1997

Chas Debenham

THE BLACK BUOY, *WIVENHOE*

This picture shows the side of The Black Buoy in Wivenhoe.
I painted it in the mid-1990s with my back hard up against the
wall of a house and all my paints lying at a convenient height on
top of a wheelie-bin. An interesting place to work.

It took visits over several weeks to complete the painting,
and often I was privy to a university lecture. These are very low
houses and, like the open window of the pub, I had an window
open a few feet above me. One of Wivenhoe's world experts
was practising his lectures, probably on his wife or girl friend, full
volume for the benefit of anybody within range.

APPROACHING SNOW, *WIVENHOE*

This was painted in the mid-1990s in Anglesey Road, one of
those unadopted roads full of pot-holes, awkward to drive
down. While I was painting this, the sky changed dramatically,
swirling deep blues and fantastic greens suddenly appeared, and
I got the title for this picture.

LEAVENHEATH POST OFFICE AND CONVENIENCE STORE

Often my chosen vantage point has singular disadvantages. This view was painted from the top of the petrol storage tanks, and the resulting fumes were not the worst of it. Try standing on a metal plate for four or five hours at a time, during December (including Christmas Day) and January. There was also the interruption of unofficial extra duties. As well as pump inquiries, I also doubled as used-car representative. A small Portakabin-style office was to the side of me, unmanned most of the time. There were about a dozen or so cars on either side, and I was the only visible contact.

Originally, this subject caught me eye as I was coming from the road in the opposite direction. Then I saw the apparent red sofa, which is actually a self-service bin for bagged fuel, and the flowers, looking colder than I felt. The two red cone-shaped things covered fire extinguishers.

Like many similar businesses, this one was struggling. First, one of the pumps ran dry, then one Sunday all the bundles of newspapers and milk remained stacked on the doorstep, a trickle of customers came and tried the door, then as a last resort came over to me, yet another unofficial duty. The convenience store was still for sale over a year later.

Exhibited: Royal West of England Academy, 1999

Chas Debenham

Chas Debenham

PINECRAFT, *NORTHWOLD*

Summer 2000, and after spending an entire morning reconnoitring mostly on foot villages around the A134, I ended up in Northwold. By the time I had finished drawing Pinecraft it was late afternoon. Time to go into the shop – it's got one of those bells that ring when you open the door – and introduce myself to the owner, Pam.

"I'm the guy parked over there painting a picture of your shop," I explained. It was doubly a reassurance that I was not a stalker, or planning a raid. "Please don't tell me you are going to do any decorating outside for the next few weeks. I noticed that there are touches of undercoat on the door... and please don't do any weeding."

Pam was understanding. I was assured that there would be no immediate repainting. She herself paints, but only when on holiday in the Greek islands. "However, we will have to do some weeding. My mother has just died and the shop has to look tidy for the funeral, next week."

I was back in just two days, after allowing for the drawing paint to dry. Now I faced the problem of painting from the bottom up, weedy foreground first, one of those arse-about-face jobs. As if I needed reminding how fast I had to work, all I could hear most of the day was the agitated clicking of someone hoeing a drive or stony garden.

WINTER GARDEN, *GODDARD'S CORNER, NEAR WIX*

Upgrading the Harwich road had created a good safe position for me in the old road, now serving only this small cluster of houses. The picture was painted in 1999.

I was fascinated by the basic nature of these agricultural cottages and the tin sheds, knocked up by the tenants, now showing beautiful patterns of rust.

This is a winter view, when everything has almost gone back to nature. Look at the tall grass, the unattended flower beds, the vegetable plots with last year's crop running to seed, nothing growing and the soil still to be retilled.

CEDAR COTTAGE, *HORRINGER*

This cottage, with its patterned chimneys and eyebrow windows looking out at you as if saying: "Please come and re-thatch me," was originally part of the Ickworth estate, just outside Bury St Edmunds. Louise Ward is standing in front of her cottage which takes its name from an enormous cedar tree that stands just out of view, on the right. I would just love one like it in my garden.

The chap who kindly let me block his drive on the days I was painting asked: "Why don't you paint my house? It used to be the old workhouse."

REPAIRS TO THE CHURCH TOWER, *BOXFORD*

Boxford is typical of the Essex-Suffolk border. It is a nice little town. I've painted here before, but I would not want to live here with my door opening on to the street, with bumper-to-bumper parking. I don't think a single local artist missed the intruder on their patch.

The tower looked as if it had been plastic-wrapped by the artist Christo – maybe a bit more decoratively than he would have done it! A few years before they restored the tower, they did the porch, losing all the lovely naturally acquired patina. During restoration it was sand-blasted and came out very raw, much more than I show it.

SHEILA, JOCK AND MAC, *STONE STREET*

You never spot anything to paint in Stone Street if you just drive through. The whole place is one narrow, twisting road, pedestrians tread carefully and cars sort out who's got preference. I painted this in 1999 from the safety of a derelict garden, protected from traffic and people by a thick, wide hedge.

Sheila, Jock and Mac are passing Graham K Beeton's Electrical & Plumbing Supplies. Graham has left the scene now, the last in the line of businesses on this site which included Antiques & Fine Art, a Curtain Exchange, a bookshop and a grocer's.

TOOL HIR

Chas Debenham

PROCTOR'S SHOE SHOP, *WYMONDHAM*

I was caught hiding up a small passage-way by the butcher's, while painting Proctor's Shoe Shop. The mumsy lady politely ushered her young son and daughter between me and the easel. "They're really very interested in art," she explained, then she pointed out the technical bits. "See how he's left out all the scaffolding." Scaffolding, what scaffolding? "Oh *that* scaffolding, no dear, I'm painting the other corner."

List of illustrations
by page number

Charles Debenham Exhibitions

Mixed exhibitions include:

Royal Academy, London; Mall Galleries, London; Royal West of England Academy, Bristol; South West Academy, Exeter; City Museum & Art Gallery, Gloucester; Beecroft Art Gallery, Westcliff-on-Sea; Adam Gallery, Bath; Castle Museum, Colchester; Chelmsford & Essex Museum; Epping Forest District Museum, Waltham Abbey.

Solo exhibitions include:

The Minories, Colchester; Digby Gallery, Colchester; Gainsborough's House, Sudbury; Quay Theatre, Sudbury; Chappel Galleries, Chappel.